PORTLAND TO SAN FRANCISCO
ON THE PACIFIC COAST ROUTE

Bicycling Great Places

David E. Siskind

Books About Bicycling
Minneapolis, Minnesota

PORTLAND TO SAN FRANCISCO
ON THE PACIFIC COAST ROUTE

Bicycling Great Places

David E. Siskind

Published by:
Books About Bicycling
5812 Thomas Circle
Minneapolis, MN 55410
612-929-0205
dsiskind@earthlink.net

ISBN 978-0-9678878-8-3

Covers
Front: Eamon and Meghan waiting until it is safe or at least safer) on an Oregon coastal bridge.
Rear: The author and his Rivendell bike.

Previous Books About Bicycling titles:

1. Bicycling the Adventure Cycling Northern Tier Trail Across America, Tour Story of Two Sometimes Grumpy Old Men. 2000, 6x9, 74 pages, illustrated

2. Bicycling the Canadian Rockies, A Planning Guide and Stories of Seven Trips. 2002,6x9, 112 pages, illustrated

3. You Started From Where? Bicycling 420,000 Miles From Pennsylvania to Minnesota. 2004, 8-1/2x11, 380 pages, illustrated

4. Bicycling Alaska, Two Coasts, Three Michigans and the Natchez Trace, Bicycling Great Places. 2011, 8-1/2x11, 206 pgs, Illustrated

5. Route 66 By Bicycle, Bicycling Great Places. By David E. Siskind and Thomas O'Brien, 2012, 6x9, 75 pages, illustrated

6. The Great Allegheny Passage and C & O Canal, to Toronto, Bicycling Great Places. 2012, 6x9, 55 pages, illustrated

6a. The Great Allegheny Passage and C & O Canal, Pittsburgh to Washington, DC, Bicycling Great Places. 2013, 6x9, 83 pages, illustrated

7. A Short Bicycle Tour in the Netherlands, Bicycling Great Places. 2014, 99 pages. Illustrated

Available from booksaboutbicycling.com and from Amazon.com

PORTLAND TO SAN FRANCISCO ON THE PACIFIC COAST ROUTE

A LONG RIDE TO AN UNKNOWN DESTINATION

You never know what will be the memorable moments on a bike tour. Like getting on a vintage trolley car in San Francisco not knowing where it's going. The driver was ushering the crowd aboard and I joined them. Nobody around me could tell me what the deal was, where we were going, why no fares were collected, or if we'd return to Fisherman's Wharf.

My memory took me back almost 70 years as a child in Philadelphia when I rode the old Castor St. trolley before it became a rubber-tired "trackless" bus-trolley. I had loved trains then. As we cruised along San Francisco's Market Street, riders were exiting and still not paying. I wondered if I'd end up in the car barn, parked there overnight. But for some reason, I was enjoying the ride too much to be worried. I did finally ask the driver and he reassured me we'd be returning to Fisherman's Wharf, like, that same day (whew!). It was a great way to see the city, it's people and it's culture and for only 75¢ (senior rate). I asked when I got off and that's what it cost me. My particular car was labeled Cincinnati. I had noticed on my 2010 visit that these rail-running trolleys were from all over including my hometown of Philadelphia.

THE TOUR PLAN

My recent long summer tours have followed the July Winnipeg Folk Music Festival (that being a family tradition since 1989): British Columbia's mountains, The Canadian Rockies, Prince Rupert, The Oregon Sierra's, the California coast and, on the other coast, Nova Scotia and Newfoundland. This year, my daughter Lisa suggested I visit her in Corvallis where her husband is taking OSU graduate courses. Also on my permanent want-list is to see and bike with my longtime biking partner, Tom O'Brien in Portland. And thus, a tour was born.

The plan was to visit Tom, bike south along the Willamette River to Corvallis, see Lisa and Joe, then turn to the coast somewhere around there. Then I'd go down the Oregon Coast to California, turn east to do Adventure Cycling's Sierras route to Tahoe and finally take the Western Connection to San Francisco. Figuring I would need it in the Sierras, I had full camping gear including extra clothes for cold and a warmer sleeping bag than I'd had on the CA coast in 2010. The first part went as planned but the Sierra mountain route in California was abandoned on account of weather and wildfires. I did still end in San Francisco but it was via the coastal route I'd done in 2010 plus a major side trip to Sacramento.

MINNEAPOLIS TO WINNIPEG, MANITOBA, CANADA

I had concerns and that seems the norm these recent years for a guy in his 70's. There were health issues plus a lack of much biking because of a winter that wouldn't quit in Minnesota, like significant snowfalls in April. It was enough for me to add 3 days to what used to be 6-1/2 days, six of them being Centuries. I was glad for the extra time as I had stiff north (headwinds) almost all the way. There were days I was down to 8 mph and considered quitting early. This was my 19th time biking to Winnipeg on the more-or-less direct route and my 25th time doing any which way.

En route, I had a couple of brief showers and one too-close camper passing me that had me shaken and angry. The first day to St. Cloud was 85 miles and gave me confidence that I could do it despite strong headwinds. I tried to camp on Day Two in Little Falls, MN, but swarming mosquitos chased me to a local motel. I didn't try camping again until Winnipeg and the music festival campground. As it was, I could have let my wife Dana bring up the tent, pad and sleeping bag when she drove up. I would still need it out west.

I used several of Minnesota's long-distance and paved bike trails and then the quiet roads in the sparsely populated north of Minnesota and into Manitoba. Highlights were a wonderful Chinese buffet in St. Cloud, sitting lakeside in Bemidji for the 4th-of-July fireworks, visited old friends, Harold and Shirley in the tiny northern town of Oklee, MN, and managing to turn three of my days into Centuries.

A BAD BANK

Another reason to be turned off about banks these days. The one in St. Milo, Canada wouldn't exchange US cash for Canadian money. They said it was because I didn't have an account with them. They had done it for me since 1989 so this was both annoying and, I thought, really stupid, How am I supposed to have an account in a Canadian bank? They said I could go to a train station or airport. Sure, I'll hop on my bike and do just that. Luckily, I had some Canadian money from last year. And luckily, a credit union in Landmark exchanged money for me the next day.

AT THE FESTIVAL

As I usually do, I biked every day while at the festival. I took the park paths and circle road to and from the showers and the camp store for coffee and a muffin in the mornings and to and back from the day and evening performances. Recently, it seems there's about as many bikes as cars in the festival parking.

One morning was my traditional ride to the town of Selkirk, 14 miles distant, for breakfast. I pushed it a bit to get back in time to line up for the 10:30 gate opening. The festival usually has great performers who we have never heard of before and maybe one well-known personality. This year there were more famous names: Bonnie Raitt, Buffy Sainte-Marie, Ani Di Franco and Joan Baez and a special tribute to Pete Segar.

TO NORTH DAKOTA AND AMTRAK TO PORTLAND

I had three days to get to Grand Forks, ND to catch my Amtrak train ride to Portland. It was lucky that I managed to do the biking in two as Amtrak threw a monkey wrench into my plans. I'd need that third day. That strong north wind I had fought for nine days was still blowing as I headed south at 18+ mph. It was obvious that I could make the 106 miles to Hallock so that's what I did. (I gave myself a high-five.) With the town's three hotels full (of pipeline workers), I was glad I had my tent (another high-five). While in the city park, two dusty motorcycles pulled in. It was a young couple that had come from Alaska.

At the border, I had another interesting border guard encounter. Most and certainly worst I've had were in reentering into the USA. They asked me how long I had the bike and wanted its serial number. Having 19 bikes in all, I didn't exactly recall that my first miles on the Rivendell were in 2005 although it had been ordered 18 months earlier. I later wondered if what brought this about was because the bike looked new despite have gone 34,000 miles and was in Canadian flag colors. Really. Why would anyone go to Canada to buy a bike? Everything in Canada costs more. What were they thinking?

The next day was a "cakewalk" to Grand Forks, North Dakota, 78 miles. I picked a motel close to the train station and then biked there to find out about a bike box. I had a plan B to get one from a local bike shop if needed. The station agent said he had a box. That was the good news. The bad news was that Amtrak was using buses instead of trains from Fargo to Minot (west of Grand Forks) and he couldn't guarantee that they would be able to accommodate my bike. I biked GF's bike paths back downtown to do the riverside trails and rack up another Century while pondering what to do.

There was a precedent for this situation. Tom and I had to rent a van to get to Chicago for our East Coast tour in 2007 when the same Amtrak Empire Builder was bussing because of a track washout between St. Paul and Chicago. The solution was similar now - rent a car and drive to Minot. That's how I used my third day: a morning ride in Grand Forks, a 200-mile drive, and some local biking in Minot.

There was a bright side: I was supposed to get on the train, bike all boxed up, in Grand Forks at 4:52 a.m. I wasn't sure how I'd manage that. With my driving to Minot, the train departure would be after 9:00 a.m., That allowed me to stay in a hotel, get up at a reasonable time, have breakfast, bike to the station and do the box thing. And they did have one (I had checked). This was yet another high-five. These are a lot more satisfying when a second person is involved but you do with what you have, I guess.

I had ridden the Empire Builder train west before but from St. Paul. It's a long drag, but this time I had one instead of two overnights. Amtrak handles bikes far better than flying and costs much less - only $10 plus $15 for the box if a new one is needed. And, unlike flying, I have never had damage with either Amtrak or the Canadian counterpart, Viarail. My biking mileage total for this tour so far in Minnesota, Manitoba and North Dakota was 1,103.

OREGON WITH OLD BIKING PARTNER TOM O'BRIEN

Tom met me at the station with his bike. We did the Sunset Highway (US 26) over the west hills and then back roads to his and Lois's house. Still early, the traffic and the heat during the climb weren't too bad. My daughter Lisa joined us for dinner that evening. She was working that summer in Portland and I would later see her and her husband Joe in Corvallis. Tom and I had two days of local riding (33 & 40 miles) and a wonderful visit. Tom has done almost all of my long tours including our Coast-to-Coast, Adventure Cycling Northern Tier in 1998, Route 66 in 2003, the Yukon and Alaska in 2004, The Atlantic Coast, and the Natchez Trace ride of 2008.

I had seen Tom and biked with him last August (2013) just as he was finishing up his cancer treatment. He says he has good and bad days but that wasn't evident to me last year nor again now. Either that or I am not aware of how much my own speed has declined.

I regret that we will likely never do another long tour together but have the consolation, weak by comparison, that I can relive the ones we did do in my writings. It's tough getting old. Tom's wife Lois

8

worries a lot about him when he rides. He has health issues, more so than me, and is, after all, 76 years old. It therefore came as a surprise when he said he'd ride with me for the first two days of my tour. I was joyful at this as Tom is the best riding partner one could wish for.

We biked to Salem, 54 miles, over hills the biggest I'd done yet this season. Towns we passed through were Murray Hills, Newberg, St. Paul and Keizer on a mix of roads and bike paths. We could see smoke to the east from wildfires and brief views of Mt. Hood. We were basically following the valley of the Willamette River and had no mountains to cross. Salem is the state capital and I took a short ride downtown to check it out.

The next day was to Corvallis, 43 miles. We had wet pavement to start and moderate headwinds but we took it easy again on a combination of roads and bike paths. This was part of Adventure Cycling's Trans-Am route via towns of Rickreall, Monmouth, Adair, & Lewisburg. Paved bike paths seem to be proliferating in Oregon and not just in larger towns with Universities. I believe these four days were Tom's longest rides of the year, to date. We both felt happy and satisfied this evening.

The next day's rain frustrated our plans. I was to bike part way back to Salem with Tom where Lois was to pick him up. The rain didn't stop until it was too late for any biking so Lois drove all the way to Corvallis to retrieve Tom. It was a sad but inevitable parting. At least I had a dry evening to visit with Lisa and Joe, see their house, have dinner and walk the campus of Oregon State University (OSU), where Joe is taking grad courses. We also went to a movie. It was a busy evening and a nice visit.

HEADING TO THE OREGON COAST

I don't like days off on a bike tour, like I'd just had. With the bit in my teeth, I was more-than ready to roll. The best-appearing route to the Oregon coast was from Eugene so that town was my goal for this day. Still on the A.C. route southbound, I went through Harrisburg and Coburn (What's with these names? These are Pennsylvania towns.) Eugene was a very busy place, home of The University of Oregon. I explored downtown and the campus but riding only became fun when I found their bike path system that run both both east and west of town. Most of this is riverside or creekside. It was also a chance to preview my ride of the next day, west toward the coast.

In my exploring, I accidentally ran across the Bike Friday Company plant and showroom. I was welcomed despite not, at the moment, riding my own Bike Friday - old, SN 188 bought in 1992. I was given a VIP tour by Peter Berra and told to call him if I ran into difficulties. These amazing people and their company were a trip highlight. I couldn't seem to quit this day, making a 44-mile day into 102 and lasting until 9 p.m. (The following winter, I ordered a Bike Friday for my wife Dana.)

The ride from Eugene to the coast is an alternative A.C. Trans-Am route. Westbound, it was a back road through Crow to Neti, a quiet and nice 27 mi, and then Hwy. 128 to Florence. This was 69 miles in all. Peter from Bike Friday said that route was nasty and Tom has always said the roads connecting the Willamette Valley and the Coast were dangerous. I found it had lots of traffic but a good shoulder. One steep climb was to 769ft and then an easier one to a tunnel. The wind became fierce nearing Florence - off the ocean, down from the NW and cold. The idea of camping lacked appeal. I found a cheap hotel and dinner on the main drag, which was Hwy 101. Later I discovered Florence's quaint & historic downtown.

THE OREGON COAST - SOUTHBOUND FOR SAN FRANCISCO

Just out of Florence, I met John and Bill from the Bay Area and heading south to there. They were about my age but faster than I wanted (or could) go. In fact, John was going faster than Bill apparently wanted to go. So I let them go. I then joined up with Eamon and his college-age daughter Meghan from Vancouver. They were going to San Diego but, in the meantime, struggling with Meghan's nonfunctioning gearshift lever. A screw had been sheared off and it wasn't a roadside fix. She was managing the not-insignificant hills without being able to shift her rear gear. I envy the strength of the youth.

I biked with them from just outside of Florence to Reedsport for a second breakfast and then to a North Bend bike shop where Megan's shifter was replaced. The route then left US 101 for one closer to the coast. The views were okay but the road wasn't much fun being too busy and with a marginal shoulder. After Charlestown was a very steep climb of 400ft requiring my lowest gear (22in) and a ton of sweat. I'd earned another self-given high-five. As I had ridden all day with Eamon and Meghan, 75 miles, I decided to camp with them at Bollard's Beach just short of Bandon, Oregon.

The hiker-biker campsite already had four other bikers. I managed to impress them all by riding into loose sand and flopping over. They all stood around as I struggled to unclip my shoes and get out from under the bike. One of the bikers was Duane Klinge whose home is about 5 miles from mine in Minnesota. He had ridden west on the A.C. Northern Tier and was now headed for southern CA. I was amazed that I had not somehow met him or at least knew of him as we both had done similar kinds of bike touring.

Another biker from California said my plan to bike the Sierras at this time would be unpleasantly hot. The Weather Channel also wasn't encouraging, showing temps at Grant's Pass expected to be in the high 90's all week, even possibly topping 100. I had to decide if I really wanted to bike up mountains in that heat.

We'd had a good day with light tailwinds to start and later stronger winds out of the north as we were biking south. I felt sorry for the few northbound bikers we saw. Between the hills out of Florence and the "wall" after Charleston was a pleasant and easy section with high sand dunes on the ocean side - This was the Oregon Dunes National Recreation Area. The only recreation I noticed from the highway was dune buggies.

Eamon, Meghan and I continued on together much of the next day. We did the Bandon Loop Road with scenic offshore rocks, to Port Orford, an easy ride. Our food-store-lunch was overlooking the cove

11

and behind a wall from the fierce, cold wind. Then we had the canyon and climb around Humbug Mountain and back to the rocky coast. Hwy. 101 was marked as a state bike route so we stayed on that rather than A.C.'s back road alternative after Ophir.

I parted from Eamon and Meghan at Gold Beach. I was conflicted and sad. Good road companions are hard to find. They were going on to Brookings, another 29 miles. If I biked there with them, my next day would have been a trivial 14 miles to Smith River. (I was still thinking that Smith River was to be my point of departure for the interior - Hwy 199 NE to Cave Junction, Grant's Pass, and east to the Sierras.) And they had a schedule to keep for Meghan to be back for school. I was still debating myself, whether to do the A.C. Sierra route or stay on the coast. If I did the coast, I had way too many days and would have to cut my daily mileage or do some big side trips. (I ended up doing both.) I had anticipated this might happen and was prepared with A.C. maps for both routes.

I liked what I saw of the Oregon coast, the southern half. It was hilly with about 20 approximately 400-ft climbs and four of about 800 ft. The route profile looks like a comb. There were some sections with minimal to no shoulder and lots of traffic including trucks hauling cut lumber. On the good side, it's a spectacular and scenic ride that attracts bikers worldwide. For me, the ocean side rocks, cliffs, beaches and vistas were awesome and the air clear, until close to Brookings anyway.

The state parks have hiker-biker sites eliminating the worry of arriving and being turned away. And they were only $5.00. The wind could be fierce and was generally out of the north. Most bikers were wisely southbound. Also and in general, there is little rain until mid-September. There are possibly several hundred bicyclists doing this every season, most using the AC route maps. I speculated to myself that the motorists on this coastal route might be used to seeing bikes, accounting for the relatively few overly close passes. I know experienced Minneapolis area bikers who'd tried this and didn't like it, presumably because of the narrow and busy roads. By contrast, I hope to someday bike the northern half in Oregon that I've never done.

MY BIG DECISION MADE – NOT THE SIERRAS

I was still undecided as I rolled out of Gold Beach, Oregon and then immediately up the grueling 800-ft climb on a full stomach. I had to stop every 1/2-mile of the 2-1/2 mile climb for a short breather. Another sign of my age, I guess, in addition to being generally slower.

There were nice sea stacks south of Cape Sebastian State Park but I had fog the rest of the way to Brookings. I guess I had subconsciously made my decision as I biked past Smith River and on to Crescent City. Now I was on familiar ground. I had been here in 2010 when I had biked from Vancouver and did the Sierra Cascade route in Oregon that included Hood River, Detroit, Bend, Crater Lake, Grants Pass (A chapter in my book Bicycling Alaska, Two Coasts, Three Michigans and the Natchez Trace, Bicycling Great Places. 2011.)

I also became aware about this time that they were having serious wildfires in the Sierras where I had intended to go. However, by staying on the coast, I'd have to deal with the fact that I had 18 days for the 400 miles to SF. Even with the hills and my feeling less than stellar, it was about 10 more that I'd need. It was no big surprise that I'd have no problem filling these days.

MEETING, CAMPING AND RIDING WITH OTHER BICYCLISTS

I had been a physical scientist. My primary interests have been landforms, geology, technology (bicycle and otherwise), and the environment. History is secondary and botany a distant third. That's why my bike tour stories include little on history and less on the plants and animals encountered. Finally, for sociability, I have my wife and, when on tour, Tom.

So I was surprised to realize how significant to me were my encounters with other bike tourists, despite these being invariably temporary and fleeting. In addition to those met in Oregon were many more in California, mostly encountered in the hiker-biker campsites. The Pacific Coast is a popular Adventure Cycling route. I camped with some and rode with them. Actual companionship on the road was short as most were younger and faster than me. Unlike my dozens of past tours, I didn't seem to have the strength to muscle up the climbs. I was thankful I had that third small chainring and I was using my two lowest granny gears (22 and 25-in) more than ever. I pondered if it was normal for my age of 72-1/2 or something else like the meds I was taking or other health issues. I could do the distance but not the speed.

In an Orick, CA restaurant, I met "The Trio," a California guy (Bodgan) riding with two beautiful (and strong) young women from Montreal (Mathilde & Benedicte). I'd see them several times including in the Gualala Campground before I left the coast for my two-day side trip to Healdsburg. Near Jenkins was a guy who had ridden from Nebraska and was heading to San Diego to live. He swore this would be his last bike tour.

In the Standish-Hickey CG, I met John from Oakland with his two-chainring Surly bike. I camped with him the following two nights but couldn't keep up with him on the climbs. With his lack of a low-gear granny ring, he had to muscle up them. He was also young (at 29) and could do that.

There was a youth group I enjoyed seeing, first in Burlington Camp and several times later. This was Apogee from Eugene with about a dozen kids and two leaders. This was a serious challenge for those kids and they were doing great. One of their group had crashed on a steep downhill near Del Rio and was suppose to rejoin them later. I last saw them at the Standish-Hickey CG but somehow felt they were close by. Two days later, in Gualala, I heard the sirens of ambulances racing north and had a sinking feeling it might be for one of them. I never did find out.

And then there was Thomas doing his first bike tour, solo for 4 days. I predict this Bay Area youth will be doing many more as he liked it and had well prepared for the experience. I camped with him on the windy spit at Bodega Bay. These short, intense and almost inevitably temporary friendships are typical of long-distance bike tours, especially on A.C. routes. You exchange e-mail addresses and ask them to let you know how their tour went. Some respond but most don't. Most I send copies of my books.

THE CALIFORNIA COAST

Adventure Cycling's Pacific Coast route from the Oregon border to San Francisco has two roughly equal length sections. The north part is mostly US 101, busy most times and most places but with a good shoulder. This 183-mile stretch has a few excursions, side roads, and one long and wonderful 30-mile Avenue of the Giants. The southern half is exclusively coastal CA Hwy. 1 until the approach to the Golden Gate Bridge in Marin County.

The coastal bike route continues to be hilly with three 1,000-ft climbs, the first after Crescent City (in Del Norte Coast Redwoods State Park), another approaching Garberville on US 101, and a final one after Leggett preparing you for the 2,000-ft descent to the coast and CA Hwy. 1. My copy of this map section wasn't A.C.'s latest and it didn't have the route profile and some route changes. Sometimes perhaps, it's better not to know and therefore not to worry. Like Tom has said, "You get to it, you do it," and "Shift down and grind it out." In addition to those climbs, there were scores of smaller ones although for this old guy, many didn't seem as small as they were 4 years earlier.

One thing the same as the 2010 tour was the cold, wet wind off the ocean. I froze when camping back then with my old summer-weight sleeping bag. I was better equipped this time, both bag-wise and with extra nighttime clothes (long sleeves and a warm hat). Another similarity was the coastal fog almost every day and all day. I used my flashing head and tail lights a lot.

California's northernmost town is Crescent City. After that one big climb, a second lesser one and an easy stretch came the first excursion off 101, Newton B. Drury Parkway within Prairie Creek Redwoods State Park. This starts with a pretty steep 1.5-mile climb. Then follows 6-1/2 miles of gentle downhill through a forest of huge

15

trees, some right alongside the road. It's like bicycle paradise. But then it's back onto 101. Then came more hills, Orick where I first met "The Trio," and then my overnight this day at Patrick's Point Inn. This is a nice place where I'd stayed in 2010, except that dinner is 5 miles away in Trinidad. But as I have often said, "It all counts." Eureka was a milestone plus also being a short and easy 34 miles. Off of 101, on back roads through McKinleyville and Arcata, I was in farm- and pastureland. A hotel search was interesting. The first I found was even below my standards and the one where I settled barely made them. I'd biked across town three times: to find AAA for a map I'd need for my Healdsburg excursion, to do laundry, and to see the old historic downtown plus a little exploring. I saw The Trio in town searching for a bike shop and then planning to go onto Burlington Camp, my next day's planned overnight.

REDWOOD TREES ON THE AVENUE OF THE GIANTS

My vacation in Eureka was over. On the plus side, I'd gain the beautiful, warm and dry redwood forest in place of the cold, windy and foggy coast. But I had a lot of work ahead before the Burlington Camp in Humbolt Redwoods State Park. It wasn't until I was doing them that I remembered how wasted I was doing this stretch in 2010. The first hill was near Loleta and then three times going up and then back down again between Fernbridge and Rio Dell with the Eel Valley visible below. More than ready for lunch (and a rest) in Rio Dell even though only 10:00 and with only 29 miles done. Momentarily stopped, I was greeted by John and Bill (from 6 days earlier) across the fence on Hwy. 101. I suspect their ride had been a lot easier.

Then came the good ride, onto the 30-mile Avenue of the Giants. This passes through Humbolt Redwoods State Park and includes the wonderful Burlington Camp. More paradise. It is so dark under those big trees that nobody drives fast. It is almost impossible to bike this route and not stop at one or both of these campgrounds, unless perhaps you don't have food with. (I had earlier picked up a sub. There was no food available in or near the Humbolt SP campground.)

16

I was later joined by the Apogee youth group under those giant trees.

The next day's ride was the rest of "The Avenue" and then to a real breakfast in Miranda. I remembered this restaurant where in 2010, I lingered with my coffee while a German biker I had camped with the night before finished his breakfast. He then took off, leaving me in the dust. Oh well.

After the AOTG came a memorable (but not exactly pleasant) 10-mile stretch on Hwy. 101. I saw the Apogee Group at this junction, paused, and doing coordinated hydration-upon -command. The riding is easy along the South Fork of the Eel River but then, approaching Garberville, starts to seriously climb. Not steep but hot, no shade, and the wind behind for real sweat-hog experience. I wondered if this is what it would have felt like if I had done the Sierras. It was incredibly scenic but hard to enjoy under those conditions. I kept looking behind, expecting to see the Apogee kids coming along (and to maybe shoot some photos) but they didn't appear until later when I'd stopped for lunch in town.

The downhill, when it came, gave me a trip high of 44 mph. The rest of the way to Standish Hickey State Recreation area and CG was a mix of CA highways 271 and 101. Being next to each other and intertwined, I assumed 271 is the old highway and 101 the freeway replacement. Very nice but by Confusion Hill at 43.5 miles and 1:30 p.m., I was toasted, tired, and likely depleted. I had thought, apparently wrongly, that my Subway stop only 21 miles earlier had been enough. More food and a brief rest helped. I knew camp was only another 5-1/2 miles and in the deep and wonderful forest. I later found that local temps had reached 96. That explained a lot.

In the CG that evening was the duo of John and Bill (again) and a younger John from Oakland (the 29-year-old), doing the Coast to home. This John and I camped together the next two nights. I couldn't match his uphill speed and so we didn't go down the road much together. The Apogee group had arrived too but didn't join us in the hiker-biker site. By evening in Standish-Hickey, I had recovered enough for an exploratory ride, 3 miles, to Leggett. I wanted to know if that could be a breakfast place. The answer was "no," not even coffee in the gas station.

THE ROUTE LEAVES US HWY 101 FOR COASTAL CA HWY 1

John and I were up by 6:00. The other John (with Bill) was already gone. We were leaving US 101 for CA 1. I knew we had a big downhill from Legget and A.C. recommended doing it early to avoid traffic. But I had forgotten that a big climb came first (about 1,000ft up), and then the 1,900-ft descent. Although, in theory, I was riding with John, that didn't include the climb where he powered on ahead. The descent wasn't much fun either, mostly too winding to really let it roll. Once down, I expected a coastal ride but instead there followed another big climb. The twisty line on the map should have been a clue. By Westport, 30 mi, I needed to stop for food. John didn't and went on ahead.

Fort Bragg looked interesting and a good place to hang out. I was tired enough to consider it even with only 45 miles done. I remembered feeling this way in 2010 too and, like then, sought a motel. Rooms were scarce and the one I found that was available was $227. Also like in 2010, I said (to myself) "screw that," and rolled on. No way Jose, especially not when the H-B campsites are only $5.00. Besides, it was too early. I was the first biker at the Van Damme State Park Hiker-Biker site but then John (29) rolled in. I had apparently passed him in Fort Bragg. We hiked up the hill for dinner in the local deli. An upscale inn was there too and that was to be our breakfast buffet the next morning (a Sunday).

Morning: drip, drip, drip on the tent. It wasn't rain but the dew descending like a very fine shower and the drips were from the tree above. John and I packed up and biked up to the inn. It wasn't a buffet but big enough and busy. We didn't get on the road until 10:00, about 3 hours later than I like.

I had decided to do a side trip up the Navarre River to another redwood forest (a 17.5-mi round trip). The road was, as expected, easy, dry, sunny, and deeply forested. Not expected was that half the traffic from CA Hwy 1 was on this road, presumably a shortcut to

101 and to the Napa Valley. I hadn't anticipated this. I guessed most were homebound on this, a Sunday. John had gone on and we said we'd (probably) meet up later.

Back on CA 1 there was, as I'd expected, far less traffic. Some stretches have many stream crossings. There, the road turns inland, descends, crosses a short bridge and climbs back up. The idea was to take the downhill part and the bridge as fast as possible for the coming uphill. At least one of these was steep enough for first gear. I was having less fog and wet but stiff headwinds. I thought tailwinds were supposed to be guaranteed.

Camp was Gualala Regional Park just beyond town via an uphill and then a good downhill. There was a hiker-biker site, just like the State parks. John was there and later, the two ladies of the Trio. I biked back to town for dinner and met Bodgan there, the other Trio member.

Up before everyone else, I biked up from the CG, back down for a forgotten banana, and then back up again and to town for breakfast. Things got rough after Fort Ross with hills, one to 600ft, and zones of construction. I encountered John and the two ladies but couldn't keep up with them on the climbs and just didn't feel like trying. Bogden was behind somewhere. It was another cool, wet and headwinds day. The road also wasn't too good with no shoulder in places. As with the whole coastal ride, the drivers seemed conscious of the bikers and passed safely, mostly. The complex switch-backed road approaching Jenner was once again a source of amazement, resembling something in the Alps. I took pix of the other bikers on curves below me and across the canyon using my 20x zoom lens.

I said goodbye to the others in Jenner, probably forever, except for my plans to send them books and photos. I was staying in the inn there and to do my one- or two-day side trip to Healdsburg the next day. I had also stayed at this attractive inn in 2010 but this time considered it a bad decision. The common room was closed to guests this time, the restaurant was not open for dinner or breakfast, and my expensive room (at a "discount" of $110), had no

TV. I could have gone to a nearby CG and had this kind of service for a lot less cash.

OFF THE COAST - SIDE TRIP TO THE HEALDSBURG

This too was a repeat of 2010. Healdsburg is vineyards and wine country one valley west of the more famous Napa. It has some beautiful and quiet back roads popular with bikers and bike tour companies. The 33-mile ride to Healdsburg is along the Russian River and my easiest ride since Eugene. My motel was the same as 2010 but the cost gave me pause. She said $150 was normal but offered me a deal of $99 + tax. (It had been $145.60 for 2 nights in 2010). I took it but decided on one day and not two. After checking in, I biked Westside Road, Dry Creek Road, did laundry, enjoyed 10 minutes of their downtown park concert and biked "home" on wet streets. All this gave me a day total of 72 miles. Not bad I thought. I still had the problem of too many days. My two options were to ride south of SF on the coastal route or go east to Sacramento to bike its famous river paths. I did not have the A.C. map for south of SF but did have the one for Sacramento (The Western Express).

RETURN TO THE COAST

The next day's hotel breakfast in Healdsburg was essentially nothing, especially for $99 plus. So, got a great big one in Guerneville after 18.7 hungry miles. I also did a nice side-trip, creek-side riding from Monte Rio. Then I was back on the rocky coast again with stretches of beach and, at last, tailwinds. Not wanting to deal with the sandy Bodega Beach State Park CG where I had camped in 2010, I went on to windy and exposed Doran Park. Restless, Later, I biked the hilly way back to the Bodega Bay shops, restaurants, and the bluffs above the beaches. There I met young biker Thomas from the Bay Area who joined me at the Doran Park campsite.

For some reason, I wanted to ride alone the next morning. Probably because I wasn't feeling at my best and wanted to do exactly what I could comfortably do. Anyway, that's the way it was because

20

Thomas wasn't even stirring when I pulled out of the Bodega Bay CG at 7:00. Thinking ahead, I knew I didn't want to stay at the Point Reyes Hostel. It was too much work (a big climb), too uninviting ("Stay off the grounds until 4:00 p.m.") and too inconvenient (no food nearby). And I also recalled how nice was Samuel P. Taylor State Park when I biked through it in 2010. So that became my destination even though only 27 miles.

My plan for the rest of the tour then became: bike to San Francisco, pass through, catch the ferry to Vallejo, and then decide how far to go towards Sacramento. Then I'd return to SF. I had seven days to wander around before my two nights in SF and flight home. That way, I'd get to experience some of A.C.'s Western Express route I would have biked if I had done the Sierra Mountains.

Hwy 1 leaves the coast for the towns of Valley Ford and Tomales. Valley Ford at 9 miles was my first food and included the best cookies I have ever had - half covered in dark chocolate. The route felt like it had gotten a lot hillier since 2010. I also stopped in Tomales at 16 mi for yet more food. By contrast, the later ride along Tomales Bay was delightfully flat.

Point Reyes Station is touristy and full of what looked like day bikers from Marin County and probably SF too. I tried a restaurant there, thought it a rip-off, and went to the food store. After my picnic, a winding creek-side road took me to the Samuel P. Taylor Park's bike path. This was happy time.

I set up my tent, threw my panniers in, and biked the park paths and some of the road I'd come in on. I met Thomas heading towards the park and biked along with him. He'd decided to keep going, being close to home. I was restless and decided to bike to Languitas for both dinner and to see if it'd work out for breakfast. Seeing the post office and that it opened at 7:00 gave me an idea. Only a half-day out of San Francisco, I probably wouldn't camp again this tour so why not mail all that extra weight home the next morning?

When I got back to the campsite for the last time there were two new biker-campers. One was Mark Atherton from Woodland, CA (a town 10 miles north of Davis) and the other, a Belgian who apparently had been everywhere. I spoke at length with both but Mark (age 66) seemed to be a kindred soul. He had started his tour in Portland, biked to Astoria and then down the OR and CA coast. This was his last night out.

The next day was biking into San Francisco and, as it turned out, a lot further too. It started with breakfast with Mark in Languitas. He then went on while I did my post office business. That 10 pounds less to carry made more of a difference than I would have expected. My minimum goal this day was to not get lost in Marin County on the way to the Golden Gate Bridge. (I did miss one little turn, better than I'd done in 2010.) This took many map-check stops. I met up with Mark again in Sausalito, just by chance. We crossed the very busy GG Bridge and biked across town to the ferry terminal. He also was taking a ferry but a different one.

THE SACRAMENTO EXPERIENCE

After one-hour of inactivity on the boat, I was hyped to ride. I immediately hit the road out of Vallejo on the A.C. Western Express route. Mark told me of a better way, along the interstate, but that required some searching around. I thought maybe I'd do that coming back. I'd expected flat and it wasn't. Miles out of Vallejo, I was bonking and thinking I should have stopped there. I did finally at a Carl's Jr. at 46 miles and about 3:00 p.m. My last food had been breakfast at mile 3 and a long time and many hills ago. It was my first hot day since Minnesota. I felt pretty good despite the heat, hills and the tough winds. I spotted a motel not indicated on my A.C. map in Cordellia and could have easily quit there. But, by then, I was focused and determined on Fairfield so I motored on. One surprise was a bizarre three-way country road traffic tie-up at an all-ways stop sign.

I did have my nearly flat ride the next day but it had lots of character and was in a word, delightful. There was a valley ranchland ride between hills (Pleasant Valley Road and appropriately named), a flat one through orchards and vineyards, University of California, Davis known for its bike paths and lanes, and then more paths and lanes to Sacramento. I had done three Davis Double Centuries, 1993, 1994 and 1995, so some of that countryside looked familiar.

Davis has a Bicycle Hall of Fame. I stopped to check out the old bikes and to see who was honored. There were some I had personally known: racers Jackie Simes III and Dave Chauner, when we were all racing with the Century Road Club of America, and had encountered one way or another: John Allis when he was on the Princeton University collegiate racing team and Rich Pollini and I were on Drexel's, Keith Kingbay of Schwinn met through Fred DeLong, and Alex Moulton who visited the Twin Cities during our HPV races. Finally there were many I had known of: Major Taylor, Jack Disney, George Mount, Bobby Walthor, Barb Harmon, etc.). Not listed are some I thought deserving like Fred DeLong, Clifford Graves, Ralph Boethling and Heinz Stucke. I saw Greg LeMond honored but not Lance Armstrong. Lance and some others could have been there and I'd just missed them. The honors heavily favored racers and all seemed to be Americans. I'd decided to do a better job checking names on the way back to San Francisco but found the museum closed then.

Sacramento was new to me and turned out to be great for biking. I was told to expect hot and it was, but because of low humidity, I guess, not oppressively so. I allowed two days there so I could bike the path along the American River to Folsom, the famous prison in a Johnny Cash song. I also checked out other city paths, finding a trio of musicians jamming for fun. I couldn't resist telling them I had been at a music festival some weeks earlier, had seen some famous performers, and still had on my camera. Also fun on my two evenings was the old town with its historic buildings and wooden sidewalks. All this was easy as my West Sacramento motel was just a half-mile from the bridge to Old Sacramento.

I visited and stayed with Mark, his wife Peg, and visiting adult daughter Megan on my way back to San Francisco. I had biked back to Davis and then the 10 or so miles north through bone-dry orchard lands to Woodland. In addition to his serious biking, Mark is a craftsman with wood as shown by the projects he'd done, and will be doing for awhile, for his 125-year old home. The vegan dinner with

23

them was a new experience for me. I hope to somehow bike again with Mark. I now would have two friends living far from me who I would like to partner with for touring. Mark gave me a short tour of town before I headed back to reconnect with my A.C. route to Fairfield. My goal was the same motel as 4 days earlier. It was comforting going where I knew what to expect.

From Fairfield, I took the Linear Park Trail and then, after some construction and confusion, the road along I-80 as recommended. This included one serious climb into a 30-or-so-mph headwind. Then I was rewarded by a wonderful and welcomed descent on American Valley Rd. Fairfield-to-Vallejo via this route was only 26 miles, 9 miles less than the A.C. route I'd taken 5 days earlier. Despite the low mileage, I decided to stay here and take the morning ferry to SF. I was timing my days for my reservations in SF. I rode all around Vallejo that afternoon including a visit to the museum in the decommissioned Mare Island Naval Shipyard. My hotel that night was a clean and cheap Motel 6 with a Denny's next door. What more could a biker want?

My stay in San Francisco was a close repeat of 2010. I stayed at the Fort Mason HI Hostel, hung around the Fisherman's Wharf area and biked the wonderful shoreline paths. I also did the Daly City loop and Golden Gate Park Roads (like I had done in 2010). The mysterious trolley ride was new. I've yet to ride a cable car, visit Telegraph Hill, and bike Lombard Street.

My last day: My flight was a late one so I had time to search for the "Wiggle Route" to Golden Gate Park from Market Street. I found some memorably steep streets but finally gave up and turned south for the airport. En route, I met another old-time biker who loves and rides classic bikes, Bern Smith. Most interesting is that he had worked for legendary Phil Wood. Bern biked all the way and a little beyond the airport with me.

I had called a Burlingame bike shop near the airport and they had said they'd have a bike box for me, even a 29-er if I needed that. The plan worked, more or less. The shop gave me a box although it later turned out to be a bit small. I didn't show my chagrin, but they seemed both a little put out that I was there and totally uninterested in me, or my trip, or my bike. The Rivendell, at least, usually sparks some interest. I didn't push it and they didn't ask. Tom maybe would have pushed it. But whatever, I had a box. "Thank you bike shop." Then my biggest challenge was the box. I was holding onto it with one or preferably two hands, stretching the bungies with another and holding onto the bike with yet another. I thought of maybe going back into the shop and asking for a hand or two or three but preferred to struggle rather than go back in there. Once the collapsed box on and everything strapped down, the 3 or so miles back to the airport went without a hitch. Sun Country Airlines charged me $75 for the bike, far less than Delta would have.

A SUMMARY ANALYSIS

I did find the coastal route climbs tougher than 4 years earlier and had forgotten how much of Hwy. 1 has a minimal or totally absent shoulder. Although California is in constant geological flux, I am sure it is I that has changed. I had turned 72-1/2 years on this tour.

Unchanged from 2010 was the experience of meeting other touring bikers and having them be part of my life, even though fleeting. Still, the experience of being on the road and a new place to visit and explore each night is wonderful. I plan to continue doing this as long as I can. Perhaps with Tom, perhaps with my new friend Mark, and perhaps with my wife Dana who has rediscovered biking after retirement and doing the Great Allegheny Passage and The Netherlands. As Tom says, "Life is good."

STATS

My trip total was 47 days. That included the four-day music festival, a 1-1/2-day train ride and one rain day of zero miles (my only rain day after leaving Minnesota). I had biked 2,868 miles of which 1,100 was in Minnesota, Manitoba and North Dakota. My average from dividing the total miles by the 40-1/2 riding days was 71. I had no flats or bike troubles. It was great. I hope to do more tours although, as Tom once said while doing one unending after-arrival/exploring ride, "Dave, there is a limit."

THE TOUR DAY BY DAY

7-1 To St. Cloud, MN heading to Winnipeg, Canada. Had headwinds and a brief shower but I found shelter. Down to 8 mph near the end had me thinking of bailing out but, somehow, found the energy. Destination miles (DM) were 85 and Total Miles (TM) were the same.

7-2 To Little Falls, MN. Onto the Lake Woebegone Trail, then it was the NE extension to Holdingford. Had stiff headwinds on Hwy 10 to Little Falls. Glad for a short day. Tried to camp. DM of 53, TM of 76.

7-3 To Hackensack, MN. Hwy 371 to Brainard (32 mi), then bike trail. A celebration on the trail was ongoing in Nisswa. Headwinds again. DM: 83. Felt better after dinner and, on this nice evening, biked enough for a TM of 102 on their paved bike trail.

7-4 To Bemedji, MN. Continued on the Paul Bunyon trail including some hills requiring first gear near Walker. In Bemedji, did several trips from hotel back to downtown for local fair, to ride lakeside bike path (to its NE end), and later for fireworks. Had one brief shower on this generally nice day. DM of 52, TM of 100!

7-5 To Thief River Falls, MN. This was a real mix or hard, easy, and then miserable. Strong SSW winds made for hard going west on Hwy 2 but very nice (and fast) after turning north. Had a 2-1/2 hour visit with friends Harold & Shirley in Oklee. The remaining 29 miles to TRF was against strong N headwinds on a hot and very humid afternoon. Adding to the fun were bad rumble strips narrowing the usable road shoulder on Hwy 59 to almost nothing. Arrived late and tired. Managed to ride locally 4 miles for TM of 101.

7-6 To Karlstad, MN. Needed an easy day and this was suppose to be one. Biked straight up Hwy 59, encouraged by a light tailwind at 6:15 a.m. But, it soon turned into the all-to-common and fierce north headwind that had me down to a struggling 8 mph in my 40-in gear.

I'd been through Karlstad when up this way but had never stopped there. Nordham's Restaurant in Karlstad is also a museum of old technology, mostly printing presses and telephones. Walked around the display cases while waiting for my food. I later met a couple from Florida biking from Winnipeg to New Orleans. They mentioned the nasty afternoon the day before although, for them, it was a tailwind. This was a nice day of 70+ degrees, less windy in the evening and allowing an ambitious local ride. DM of 44, TM of 70.

7-7 To Hallock, MN. Took US Hwy 59 past Lake Bronson and then a 4-mile detour to Hallock. Later, out riding local roads and seeing a serious rainstorm approaching, I turned tail and raced back to town. DM of only 27. (At this point, I knew I had time to kill getting to Winnipeg.) My TM this day was 41.

7-8 To St. Milo, Manitoba. It was raw and headwinds to start. Had breakfast in Lancaster. Was told of very wet bikers arriving there late the day before (that must have been my evening-before's rainstorm). Hwy 59 was closed for bridge reconstruction but the workers guided me through the muddy site.

Strong headwinds had me taking a brief breather every 5 miles. That's something I previously only had to do on long climbs. (Had too many birthdays, I guess.) After checking into the town's tiny hotel, I biked in and out of the provincial park a couple of times and sat awhile reading, lakeside. DM of 50, TM of 70.

7-9 To Bird's Hill Park, Winnipeg. Headwinds (of course) but light at the start. A little bummed about heavy traffic, rough roads and strong headwinds at the ride's end and happy enough to arrive with DM and TM of 62. Dana and granddaughter Riya were already there and had set up our big tent.

7-10 to 7-13. At the Winnipeg Folk Music Festival. Did solo local riding, to and from the festival area and campground, and one traditional ride to the town of Selkirk for breakfast in a Tim Horton's. I especially like the night rides back to camp, which beats, in a big way, sitting in our van waiting for our turn to get out of the crowded parking lot. The rides these four days totaled 118 mi.

7-14 Southbound now for Grand Forks, ND. To Hallock, MN. Had expected to stop overnight in St. Milo but with glorious tailwinds, I did do two days riding in one, at 18-19 mph. Lucky, as I would later need the extra day. Camped in the city park. DM of 106, TM of 110.

7-15 To Grand Forks. Another glorious tailwind ride. After checking in to a motel, returned downtown to ride the riverside bike paths. Biked the 2 miles to the Amtrak station at 11:00 p.m. to ask about a bike box. Was told about buses being used from there. DM of 78, TM of 105.

7-16 By car to Minot, ND. Back to downtown GF for a morning ride on the riverside paths. Then biked to airport, drove a rental car to Minot (210 mi), and finally biked on local roads and across town for dinner. In all it was a full and busy day. DM of 7, TM of 60.

7-17 To Minot train station from motel. Then, all day and overnight on Amtrak's Empire Builder to Portland, OR. DM and TM of 1.

7-18 From Portland's Amtrak Station to Tom's house, with Tom: We did the usual big climb up Sunset Highway over the West Hills. This can be quite an ordeal when it is hot but early this day it wasn't. Dinner out included my daughter Lisa, in Portland this summer for work. DM and TM of 13.

7-19 & 7-20 Local riding with Tom: North Plains, Rock Creek Trail and the Bike Gallery bike shop. It was hot but okay enough. Mileages for the 2 days were 40 and 33, both being a lot for Tom these days.

7-21 To Salem, OR. On the way south with Tom on a route he had downloaded, roughly parallel to I-5. Towns were Murray Hills, Newberg, around St. Paul, and Keizer. Much traffic, some good hills & light tailwinds. Did a solo evening ride to see the Capital City's downtown. DM of 54, TM of 64.

7-22 To Corvallis, OR. Still with Tom: biked west to Rickreall to pick up Adventure Cycling's Trans-Am route south to Corvallis. Nice ride on quiet old Hwy 22, then paved bike path along Hwy 99W. To Monmouth, Adair Village, and Lewisburg. Tom later joined me in exploring the river- and creek-side bike paths in Corvallis, a University town. DM of 43, TM of 50.

7-23 In Corvallis. Rain all day and no biking. I was supposed to bike with Tom part way back to Salem. Lois arrived to pick up Tom and I spent the evening with Daughter Lisa and her husband Joe.

7-24 To Eugene, OR. Still on A.C. route. It was flat, open country, stiff headwinds, and under threatening skies that later cleared. Riding solo now. Eugene is a busy town, even scary on the streets. Did much post-arrival biking on area's paths both east and west of town (along rivers and creeks again). Visited Bike Friday Co. Couldn't quit. DM of 44, TM of 102 (crazy, obsessive, or just feeling good?)

7-25 To Florence, OR on the Pacific Coast. Crossing the coastal hills was easier than I'd expected on this alternate A.C. Trans-Am route. I had a nice 27-mi backroad to start and then rode onto Hwy 128. Then, two climbs, lots of traffic but a good road shoulder. Strong and cold winds in Florence discouraged camping. DM of 69, TM of 85.

7-26 To Bullard's Beach State Park (Bandon, OR). Met, biked with, and camped with Eamon and his daughter Meghan from Vancouver on A.C.'s Pacific Coast Route. Great tailwinds, some hills including one "wall" and sand dunes alongside the road (Oregon Dunes National Recreation Area). Busy roads with very marginal shoulders after North Bend and off of US 101. Many bikers in the hiker-biker campsite. DM of 75, TM of 83.

7-27 To Gold Beach, OR. Still riding with Eamon & Meghan. Strong tailwinds and easy riding except for the climb around Mt. Humbug. Eamon and Meghan continued on while I stopped to overnight there. These days were clear and sunny (no fog). DM of 61, TM of 77.

7-28 To Crescent City, CA. Had decided on the Coast and not the Sierra Mountain route. A tough 800-ft climb to start, more hills, heavy traffic (including logging trucks) and fog to Brookings, 30 mi. Better on back roads to Smith River and Crescent City. Was a cold, damp and headwind day. DM of 62, TM of 70.

7-29 To Patrick's Point, CA. Two climbs, the first over 1,000ft, and a harrowing descent in the fog on busy and narrow US 101. Climbing was at 5 mph and as much as 40 going down, even into a headwind. Met "The Trio," in Orick restaurant (2 gals and a guy, see the text). Biked into Trinidad for dinner. DM of 57, TM of 70. I was now on the route I'd done in 2010.

7-30 To Eureka, CA. An easy, flat ride through McKinleyville and Arcata including farmland and pastures. Then, in-town biking to see the historic old downtown, looking for AAA (for maps), and to do laundry. Saw the Trio again. DM of 34, TM of 53.

7-31 To Burlington Camp in Humbolt Redwoods State Park. Stayed on my hilly (and old map edition) A.C. route with 4 climbs off of US Hwy 101 to Rio Dell. Then, alternating deep woods and sunshine on the wonderful Avenue of The Giants (CA Hwy 254). Warm, dry and no fog up there. Apogee youth group in CG. DM of 52, TM of 62.

8-1 To Standish Hickey State Recreation Area. A real mix of road segments starting with 14 more miles on A.O.T.G. Hot on Hwy 101 to Garberville, CA 271, then back on 101 to Confusion Hill. Feeling tired and depleted at 43.5 mi. Saw John & Bill (met briefly 7 days earlier) in CG and another John from Oakland (young, by my standards, at 29). DM of 48, TM of 54.

8-2 To Van Damme State Park. Started out with John, now on CA Hwy 1. First was the 1,000-ft-climb after Legget. Then the 1,900-ft descent which was too twisty to really let it roll, and another and unexpected big climb (not fair). By Westport at 30 mi, I needed to eat but John pedaled on. Through Fort Bragg (considered the motels there) to the park and CG. Met up again with John there. DM of 59, TM of 63.

8-3 To Gualala Point Regional Park. Solo side trip into a redwood forest. Less fog but stiff headwinds when back on the coast. (not normal?) Short, steep hills at creek and river crossings. Noticed that there was much less traffic. Many must have gone home this Sunday). John and the two girls of the Trio were in the CG. I biked (alone) back to Gualala for dinner and met the other Trio member there, Bodgan. DM of 47, TM of 73.

8-4 To Jenner, CA. Big coastal rocks and beaches. Had big hills and construction zones after Fort Ross. Saw, but was unable to keep up with John and the two "Trio" girls. Bodgan was apparently somewhere behind. We all did the big switchback canyon road down and up and then onto Jenner. I stopped for the day while the others continued on. A day of low ambition for me. DM of 38, TM of 43.

8-5 To Healdsburg, CA. Two day side trip up the Russian River to wine counry plus lots of local riding on quiet roads. L&M Hotel I'd used in 2010 was expensive so I made this one overnight instead of the expected two. DM of 32, TM of 72.

8-6 To Bodega Bay, CA. Back along the Russian River to CA Hwy.1 and the rocky, windy coast. I passed busy, touristy Bodega Bay and camped in Doran Regional Park with young Bay Area biker Thomas on his first tour. Before Tom's arrival, I had returned to town for dinner and to sit on the bluff. DM of 43, TM of 62.

8-7 To Samual P. Taylor State Park. Hwy 1 swings inland to Valley Ford and Tomalis (hilly), then along Tomalis Bay (easy). Then, a riverside road to the state park's park bike path. Later biked the paths and local roads again without my camping gear and panniers. Met Mark and the Belgian in camp. It's a wonderful, forested park. DM of 43, TM of 70.

8-8 To San Francisco, Vallejo & Fairfield, CA. To breakfast with Mark. Mailed camping gear home. Through Marin County and, this time, I almost didn't get lost. Crossed the Golden Gate Bridge and biked across town with Mark. Then alone, took ferry to Vallejo and biked hill and dale to Fairfield on A.C.'s Western Express route. DM of 68, TM of 74.

8-9 To Sacramento. Scenic and easy valley ride and then along the river to Winter. From there, it was pastures, farms, orchards and vineyards. Biked through the University town of Davis, visiting the Bicycling Hall of Fame there. Then, onto the bike causeway along I-

80, and local bike lanes to the capitol city. After checking in to a motel close to downtown, I previewed Sacramento's bike paths and explored the Old Town at night. DM of 50, TM of 70.

8-10 A day of Sacramento area riding, the American River bike path to Folsom and back. Lots of bikers were out this day, a Sunday. Again hung around in Old Town. DM of 0, TM of 80.

8-11 To Woodland, CA. Back through Davis and north through bone-dry orchards to Woodland. Visited and overnighted with Mark and his family. DM of 29 & TM of 61. An explanation for that mileage is that I had further explored paths and parks in Sacramento before leaving.

8-12 To Fairfield. Hot and dry ride through the orchards to Winter. Then, nice creek-side and valley ride I'd done 3 days earlier. Exploring later, I found the Linear Park trail I'd use the next day. DM of 45, TM of 61.

8-13 To Vallejo. Biked the convenient and very nice trail, then onto a side road along I-80. it was a steep over-the-mountain climb into the wind but then a welcomed descent on American Valley road and into Vallejo. Biked around town and through the old Mare Island Naval Shipyard. DM of 26, TM of 53.

8-14 To San Francisco. Took the morning ferry from Vallejo and checked into Ft. Mason Hostel. Then, did local riding along the bay and to check out the route to the airport. DM of 7, TM of 45.

8-15 San Francisco area. Biked roads in Golden Gate Park, Pacific Coast to Daly City, and back to Fisherman's Wharf area via bayside paths. DM of 0, TM of 51.

8-16 To SF Airport via bayside bike paths, lanes and a stop at the bikeshop in Burlingame. Had a classic-riding biker escort me much of the way. Also, morning ride across town towards Golden Gate Park (didn't quite make it). DM of 24, TM of 45.

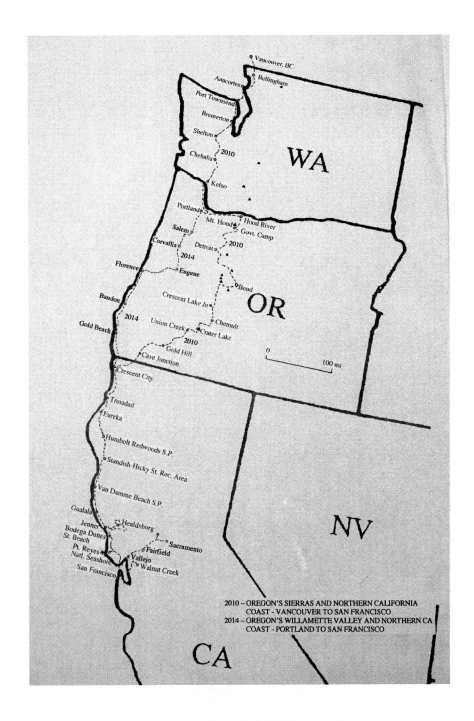

The routes of the two tours, 2010 and 2014.

1. On the plains of northern Minnesota, and Truffula-like trees.

2. The Author and his long-time riding partner, Tom O'Brien

3. A bike bridge in Salem.

4.   *The* Bike Friday factory and showroom in Eugene, OR

5.	Heniz Stuky's Bike Friday – a man well traveled.

6.	Recreation (by some measure) on the dunes along the Oregon coast.

7.   Author at bike shop in North Bend, Oregon.

8.   Meghan and her dad Eamon from Vancouver, and Dale Klinge from Minnesota in the Bullard's Beach State Park, Oregon hiker-biker campsite.

9.   Beach rocks north of Port Orford on a clear Oregon morning.

10.   Appreciated the guidance in Port Orford.

11. Coming back to the coast, southbound, after Mt. Humbug.

12. A high bridge but nothing could be seen below the deck.

13.   An Apogee youth group from Eugene, OR.

14.   A big Redwood Tree and a small cyclist.

40

15.   Redwoods on The Avenue of the Giants.

16.   High above the Eel River on US 101.

17. The store at Standish Hickey State Recreation area.

18. The CA coastal road has many ups and downs, some of about 1,000 ft.

19. Bodgan and two Canadian gals, one being Mathilde and the other Benedicte. Can you guess which end of Canada they're from?

20. California has many small beaches along its rugged coast

21. A major descent north of Jenner but before the Alpine-like switchbacks.

22. Switchbacks north of Jenner, more than are shown here.

23. Merlot vineyard near Healdsburg.

24. Young Bay area Thomas on his first bike tour.

25. Veteran California bike tourist Mark who had ridden from the start of the coastal route in Astoria, Oregon.

26. Author at the Golden Gate Bridge, San Francisco.

27. On the ferry across San Francisco Bay to Vallejo.

28. Sacramento waterfront at night.

29. Old Sacramento's shops and restaurants.

30. The long bike paths along the American River from Sacramento.

31. The San Francisco skyline from Golden Gate Park.

32. One awesome hilly town.

33. The park at Fort Mason, behind the hostel.

34. What was on the other side.

35.   Alcatraz is a big deal in San Francisco, even as a gift shop on Fisherman's Wharf.

36.   As is chocolate at Ghirardeli's in SF.

37.   Riding the vintage trolly car up Market St.

38.   San Francisco still has its
cable cars, mostly used by tourists
as if they are on a Disney Park ride.

39. Candlestick Park on its last day and also on my route to the airport.

40. A nice free breakfast is provided for hostelers.

41. Java House for a good breakfast, and for real.

42. Java House, in art.

43.   A box for the bike, on the bike.

44.   Riding is great but it is still a joy to arrive (photo by Tom).

45.   The other great joy on a bike tour: eating.